TAILS, CLAWS, FANGS & PAWS

An AlphaBeast Caper

Written and illustrated by

Terry Small

To Mary —
It was nice meeting you! I hope you find all your favorite
animals in the wild, wild pages ahead!

Best wishes,

Terry Small

A BANTAM LITTLE ROOSTER BOOK
NEW YORK · TORONTO · LONDON · SYDNEY · AUCKLAND

TAILS, CLAWS, FANGS & PAWS:
AN ALPHABEAST CAPER

A Bantam Book/March 1990

Little Rooster is a trademark of Bantam Books, a division of
Bantam Doubleday Dell Publishing Group, Inc.

Library of Congress Cataloging-in-Publication Data
Small, Terry.
    Tails, claws, fangs & paws: an alphabeast caper / written and
illustrated by Terry Small.
        p.   cm.
    Summary: Rhyming text and illustrations present a number of
animals for each letter of the alphabet.
    ISBN 0-553-05852-5
    1. Animals—Dictionaries, Juvenile.   2. Animals—Juvenile poetry.
[1. Animals.   2. Alphabet.]   I. Title.   II. Title: Tails, claws,
fangs, and paws.
QL9.S56   1990
591—dc20
[E]   89-14882
                                                              CIP
                                                              AC

Published simultaneously in the United States and Canada

Bantam Books are published by Bantam Books, a division of
Bantam Doubleday Dell Publishing Group, Inc. Its trademark,
consisting of the words ''Bantam Books'' and the portrayal of a
rooster, is Registered in U.S. Patent and Trademark Office and in
other countries. Marca Registrada. Bantam Books, 666 Fifth
Avenue, New York, New York 10103.

PRINTED IN THE UNITED STATES OF AMERICA

WAK 0 9 8 7 6 5 4 3 2 1

There's A's and there's B's, but there's nothing like these
To alarm you and charm you as quick as you please:
Some beasts to amuse, to enthuse and confuse,
And they're hardly the kind that you'll find in the zoos.

I'll guide you inside through the jungle of jaws,
Through the tails and the claws and the fangs and the paws;
We'll advance and we'll bend, we'll crawl and descend
Till we zip through the Z's at the opposite end.

Aa A is for aardvark, aye-aye, and ape,
A million amoebas without any shape;
For albatross, albacore, ant bear, agouti,
And army ant, always assigned to guard duty.

Bb B is for bandicoot, bongo, and bustard,
Bufflehead, boa, and bagworms a-clustered;
Boomslang and bobolink, badger and blenny,
And blue-footed booby, of which there aren't many.

Cc C is for copperhead, coot, cockatoo,
Curlew and conger, and cod, caribou;
Cuscus and cuckoo and Canada goose,
And cardinal, as crimson as cranberry juice.

D∂ D is for dingo and drongo and dodo,
For devil (Tasmanian) and dragon (Komodo);
For dik-dik and doodlebug, donkey and deer,
And dormouse, who dozes each day of the year.

Ee E is for elfin, echidna, and eel,
For ermine and earwig and elephant seal;
Eagle and emu and earthworm and egret,
And more whose identities must remain segret.

Ff   F is for firefly, fulmar, and fox,
Flycatcher, flounder, and flickers in flocks;
Froghopper, frigate bird, fennec, and ferret,
And four or five others without any merit.

Gg   G is for guinea pig, godwit, and goby,
For gopher, and gecko on walls of adobe;
For grampus and grunion, gorilla and grunt —
That's all you get, and it's more than you want.

Hh H is for hydra, hyena, and hyrax,
For helmeted hornbill, his face like a fire axe;
For halibut, hammerhead, hornet, and hound,
And hermit crabs holed up in houses they found.

I is for inchworm and indigo bunting,
Ichneumon, involved in his reptile-egg hunting;
For ibis and ibex and Indian skippers,
And icefish instinctively flopping his flippers.

Ii

Jj J is for jacamar, junco, and jackal,
Jackrabbit, jaguar, and jackdaws that cackle;
Jabiru, jewelfish, joey, and jay,
And jellyfish joyfully jetting away.

Kk K is for katydid, kangaroo, kite,
Kinkajou, kookaburra, kestrel in flight;
Kiwi and killdeer, koala and kudu —
I don't know more, but I'm certain that *you* do.

L is for lobster and llama and lemur,
For lemming and loon, the lunatic screamer;
Linsang and lion, loris and lynx,
And leafhoppers popping like tiddlywinks.

Mm

M is for mackerel, moose, and margay,
Marmot and marmoset, mink and moray;
Merlin and marlin, moonrat and mole,
Muskrat and mule, who can't mother a foal.

Nn N is for nightingale, nit, nematode,
And nautilus, chambered in pearly abode;
For needlefish, nanny goat, nuthatch, and noddy,
And newt — a frog trapped in a wet lizard's body.

Oo   O is for ostrich, the obvious head hider,
For oxpecker, oarfish, and orb-weaver spider;
For ocelot, osprey, okapi, and oryx,
And others so old they are all prehistorics.

P is for pewee and puffin and pigeon,
For pike, praying mantis without a religion;
Piranha and penguin and porgy and peccary —
They're spotty and stripey, but none of them checkery.

Q is for quarterhorse, harlequin quail,
Quetzal, equipped with a quality tail;
Quokka and quoll, queen bee in the hive,
And quagga of which not a one is alive.

Rr R is for razorbill, rabbit, and rail,
Rattlesnake flipping the tip of his tail;
Roadrunner, ribbon seal, rook in a rage,
And more, but I've run out of room on the page.

S is for skate and for skunk and for skink,
For scorpion, squirrel, and squid squirting ink;
Shoebill and spoonbill, sculpin and scallop,
And seahorses splashing along at a gallop.

Tt

T is for turkey and turbot and tunny,
Tenrec and toucan, with noses so funny;
Terrapin, tadpole, titi, torpedo,
And tapir attired in a tailored tuxedo.

Uu U is for unicorn, urchin, and urus,
Upside-down unai just south of Honduras;
Underwing over umbrella bird's head,
An upset uakari with face turning red.

Vv V is for vireo, vixen, and vulture,
Viper and vampire of villainous culture;
Vinegarroon, veery, and venturesome vole,
And volvox, who gather to tumble and roll.

Ww W is for warthog and woodchuck and weevil,
Wolverine, walking stick, woolly bear, weasel;
Walrus and wapiti, wahoo and wels,
And wallaby wanting to wear something else.

X is for xiphias, xenops, and xerus,
Exotic examples expected to cheer us;
For Xantus's murrelet, who flies without falling;
Extinct xiphosurans, and others still crawling.

Yy Y is for yeti and yackity yak,
For Yorkshire terrier, yellow jack;
For yamagara, yuhina, and yokel,
For yelling yapoks, and others less vocal.

Z is for zebu and zander and zibet,
Zick-zack and zibelline all on exhibit;
Zyzzyva, zoril — and that ends my chatter,
And if I knew more, this book would be fatter.

There's tails, and there's claws, and there's fangs, and there's paws;
There's bills, and there's quills, and there's maws, and there's craws;
There's wings, and there's stings — they're all in the book,
And I'm glad we're out here where it's safe just to look!

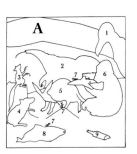

A

1. albatross
2. ant bear
3. aye-aye
4. agouti
5. aardvark
6. ape
7. army ants
8. albacore
9. amoebas

B

1. boomslang
2. bobolink
3. boa
4. bustard
5. bongo
6. badger
7. blue-footed booby
8. bandicoot
9. blenny
10. bufflehead
11. bagworms

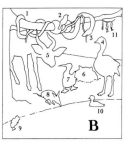

C

1. cuckoo
2. cuscus
3. caribou
4. curlew
5. cockatoo
6. Canada goose
7. copperhead
8. coot
9. cod
10. conger
11. cardinal

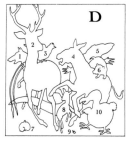

D

1. dingo
2. deer
3. drongo
4. donkey
5. Komodo dragon
6. Tasmanian devil
7. dormouse
8. dik-dik
9. doodlebug
10. dodo

E

1. elephant seal
2. elfin
3. ermine
4. emu
5. eel
6. earthworm
7. egret
8. eagle
9. earwig
10. echidna

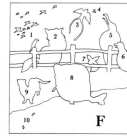

F

1. flickers
2. fox
3. flycatcher
4. firefly
5. frigate bird
6. fulmar
7. fennec
8. flounder
9. ferret
10. froghoppers

G

1. godwit
2. gorilla
3. gecko
4. gopher
5. guinea pig
6. grunion
7. grampus
8. grunt
9. goby

H

1. helmeted hornbill
2. hyena
3. hound
4. hornet
5. hyrax
6. hermit crabs
7. hydra
8. hammerhead
9. halibut

I

1. ibis
2. Indian skippers
3. ibex
4. indigo bunting
5. ichneumon
6. icefish
7. inchworm

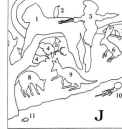

J

1. jaguar
2. jacamar
3. jabiru
4. jackdaws
5. jay
6. jackrabbit
7. junco
8. jackal
9. joey
10. jellyfish
11. jewelfish

K

1. kestrel
2. kinkajou
3. kudu
4. kangaroo
5. kookaburra
6. kite
7. koala
8. kiwi
9. killdeer
10. katydid

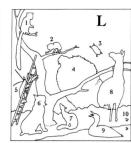

L

1. lemur
2. loris
3. lemming
4. lion
5. lobster
6. lynx
7. linsang
8. llama
9. loon
10. leafhoppers

M

1. moonrat
2. merlin
3. margay
4. marmoset
5. moose
6. marlin
7. mule
8. marmot
9. mink
10. mole
11. muskrat
12. moray
13. mackerel

N

1. nightingale
2. nuthatch
3. nematode
4. nanny goat
5. nit
6. newt
7. needlefish
8. nautilus
9. noddy

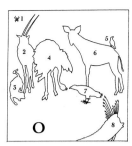

1. orb-weaver spider
2. oryx
3. ocelot
4. ostrich
5. oxpecker
6. okapi
7. osprey
8. oarfish

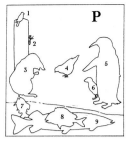

P

1. pewee
2. praying mantis
3. peccary
4. pigeon
5. penguin
6. puffin
7. piranha
8. porgy
9. pike

Q

1. quetzal
2. quagga
3. quarterhorse
4. quoll
5. harlequin quail
6. quokka
7. queen bee

R

1. razorbill
2. rook
3. rabbit
4. ribbon seal
5. roadrunner
6. rail
7. rattlesnake

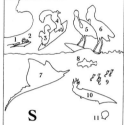

S

1. skink
2. scorpion
3. squirrel
4. skunk
5. spoonbill
6. shoebill
7. skate
8. sculpin
9. seahorses
10. squid
11. scallop

T

1. toucan
2. titi
3. tunny
4. turbot
5. torpedo
6. tadpole
7. tapir
8. tenrec
9. terrapin
10. turkey

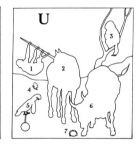

U

1. unai
2. unicorn
3. uakari
4. underwing
5. umbrella bird
6. urus
7. urchin

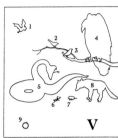

V

1. vampire bat
2. vireo
3. veery
4. vulture
5. viper
6. vinegarroon
7. vole
8. vixen
9. volvox

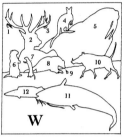

W

1. walking stick
2. wapiti
3. woolly bear
4. wallaby
5. walrus
6. woodchuck
7. weasel
8. wolverine
9. weevil
10. warthog
11. wels
12. wahoo

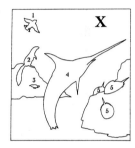

X

1. Xantus's murrelet
2. xerus
3. xenops
4. xiphias
5. xiphosurans

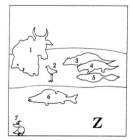

Y

1. yuhina
2. yak
3. yeti
4. yokel
5. yamagara
6. Yorkshire terrier
7. yapoks
8. yellow jack

Z

1. zebu
2. zick-zack
3. zibet
4. zibelline
5. zoril
6. zander
7. zyzzyva

GLOSSARY

Key to Glossary References

(AH) *American Heritage Dictionary of the English Language* (Boston: Houghton Mifflin, 1976).

(B&M) *Butterflies and Moths* (New York: Golden Press, 1977).

(Birds) *Birds: Their Life, Their Ways, Their World*, Dr. C. J. Harrison, ed. (Pleasantville, New York: The Reader's Digest Association, Inc., 1979).

(EB) *Encyclopaedia Britannica*, volume 18, 1948 edition (Chicago: University of Chicago, 1948).

(Macmillan) *Macmillan Illustrated Animal Encyclopedia* (New York: Macmillan, 1984).

(Mammals) *Book of Mammals* (Washington, D.C.: National Geographic Society, 1981).

(RTP) Peterson, Roger Tory, *A Field Guide to Western Birds*, Second Edition (Boston: Houghton Mifflin, 1961).

A Guide to Some of the Lesser-Known Creatures

Ant bear/antbear: alternate name of the giant anteater of South America; *Mammals* 48, 50.

Boomslang: large poisonous tree snake of Africa; *Macmillan* 452–3.

Cuscus: marsupial of New Guinea and nearby regions; *Mammals* 168–9.

Drongo: tropical bird of the Old World; *Birds* 402.

Elfin: small brown butterfly of North America; *B&M* 66–7.

Goby: small fish that attaches to rocks by a sucking disk on its belly; *Macmillan* 568–9.

Harlequin quail, Mearns's quail, or fool's quail: small quail of Mexico and southwest U.S.; *RTP* 68, pl. 22.

Icefish: shallow-water fish of Antarctica; *Macmillan* 566–7.

Indian skipper: mothlike butterfly of eastern U.S. and Canada; *B&M* 78.

Jewelfish: small freshwater fish of tropical Africa; *AH*.

Moonrat or gymnure: small mammal of southeast Asia; *Mammals* 249.

Oxpecker: African bird known for eating insects from the skin of large grazing animals; *Birds* 399.

Quokka: small wallaby of southwest Australia; *Macmillan* 24–5.

Quoll: primitive predatory marsupial of eastern Australia; *Macmillan* 16–7.

Torpedo: a bottom-dwelling ray of the Atlantic and Mediterranean capable of producing powerful electric shocks; *Macmillan* 494–5.

Unai/unau: two-toed sloth of tropical New World forests; *Macmillan* 26–7.

Uakari/ouakari: bare-faced shaggy monkey of South America; *Mammals* 385.

Wels: large nocturnal catfish of lakes and marshes from central Europe to USSR; *Macmillan* 518–9.

Xantus's murrelet or Scripps's murrelet: small, squat seabird from Siberia to California; *RTP* 110, pl. 35.

Xenops: small ovenbird of the New World; *Birds* 318–9.

Xerus, spiny squirrel, or African ground squirrel: burrowing squirrel of Africa, mistakenly thought to be poisonous; *Macmillan* 160–1.

Xiphias or broadbill swordfish: large marine fish with a distinctive long, pointed snout; *Macmillan* 570–1.

Yamagara or varied tit: small colorful bird native to Japan and Korea; *RTP* 273, pl. 60.

Yapok/yapock or water opossum: aquatic marsupial mammal of tropical America; *Macmillan* 14–15.

Yuhina: small babbler bird of Far East; *Macmillan* 340–1.

Zibelline/zibeline: rare name for the sable, a carnivorous mammal of Siberia and Japan; *Macmillan* 86–7.

Zibet/zibeth: rare name for civet of southeast Asia; *AH*.

Zick-zack or spur-winged plover: bird known for picking insects out of crocodiles' mouths; *EB* "Plover," vol. 18, p. 83.

Zoril/zorille/zorilla, or striped polecat: African mammal with skunklike defense; *Macmillan* 86–7.

Zyzzyva: tropical American weevil; *AH*.